JUL 0 1 2003

McMillan, Bruce.

The baby zoo.

$12.65

DATE		

09
30 A

Northern Koala *(Phascolarctos cinereus)* joey with its mother

THE BABY ZOO

Written and
photo-illustrated by
**Bruce
McMillan**

SCHOLASTIC INC.

New York   Toronto
London   Auckland
Sydney

With thanks to
The San Diego Zoo
and
The Saint Louis Zoo

Design by Bruce McMillan
Art direction by Claire Counihan,
Assisted by Tracy Halliday
Facts verified by Jill Gordon, St. Louis Zoo librarian
Special thanks to Veronica Ambrose,
for her meticulous copyediting
Text set in Meridien and Augustea Inline
Color separations by Color Dot
First edition printed and bound by Horowitz-Rae

ISBN 0-590-44635-5

18 17 16 15   9/9 0 1 2/0

Printed in the U.S.A.   08

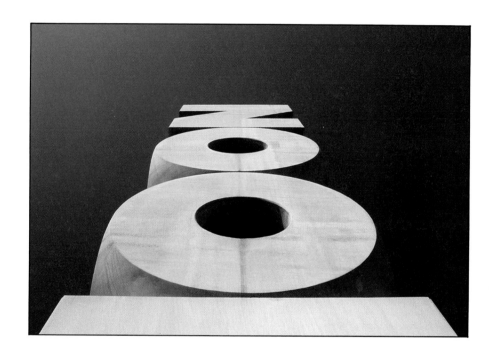

One of the baby zoo animals on the following pages wanders
freely throughout the entire zoo—not enclosed at all.
Can you guess which one?
Answer on page 40

Bawean Deer *(bah-way'-an)*

Bawean deer *(Cervus kuhli)* fawns, unlike the familiar white-tailed deer fawns, do not have spotted coats. Only male Bawean fawns eventually grow antlers. The males grow their antlers when they're one or two years old. Unlike most deer, Bawean deer bark. This is how they find each other in the forest—by barking. They hide in the forest during the day and venture out at night to feed. Bawean deer eat leaves, grass, and herbs. They are an endangered species, and it's possible they could soon become extinct. They live in the Indonesian forests on Bawean Island, located in the Java Sea between Asia and Australia.

Grevy's Zebra *(greh'-vees)*

Grevy's zebras *(Equus grevyi)* are the largest of the zebras. Within an hour after birth, newborn foals can stand and run, and thus are able to escape from animals that feed on them—predators. The newborn foals have brown stripes that become black as the foals mature and grow during their first year. Their narrow stripes and white bellies are unique to these zebras. The foals also have manes that run the whole length of their back—head to tail. Grevy's zebras were named after French President Jules Grevyi, who was given one in 1882. They live in herds, often with giraffes, ostriches, and wildebeests (also called gnus). Grevy's zebras eat thornbush and leaves of a plant called acacia, mixed with grasses. They are a threatened species, and could become an endangered species. They live in the semi-desert African regions of Ethiopia, Somalia, and northeastern Kenya.

6

Fishing Cat

Fishing cats *(Felis viverrinus)* give birth to as many as four kittens at a time, but they usually have two per litter. The kittens weigh about six ounces at birth. They first open their green eyes when they're about sixteen days old and take about eight months to grow into adults. Fishing cats are not good climbers, but they are good waders and swimmers. They show no fear of deep water. They have webbed paws. Using their paws as scoops, fishing cats crouch on rocks and scoop fish to eat. Fishing cats also eat snails, frogs, birds, and other small mammals. They live in marshy thickets, swamps, and densely vegetated areas along creeks in India, South China, and the islands of Sumatra and Java.

Spectacled Bear

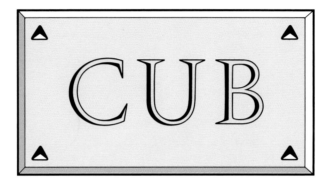

Spectacled bear *(Tremarctos ornatus)* newborn cubs usually weigh about eleven ounces. The name, spectacled bear, comes from the light-colored circles of fur around their eyes that make them look like they're wearing eyeglasses—spectacles. They are excellent climbers, often climbing trees for their primary food, which is fruit. Spectacled bears also eat the hearts and white bases of bromeliad plants, bamboo hearts, corn, and sometimes rodents and insects. These animals are a vulnerable species, and it's possible they could become a threatened and then endangered species. Spectacled bears are the only bears that live in South America. They live from Venezuela south to Bolivia in the high, humid forest regions of the Andes Mountains and, when water is available, in the coastal thorn forests.

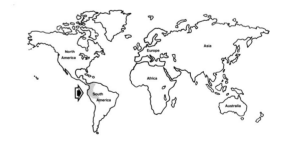

California Sea Lion

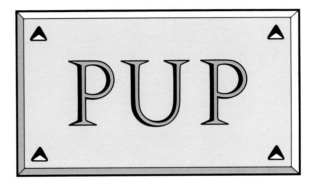

California sea lion *(Zalophus californianus)* pups are usually born in May or June in North America and from October to December on the Galápagos Islands. A newborn pup usually weighs about twelve pounds and will nurse from its mother for more than a year. Sea lions are often confused with seals. Unlike seals, sea lions have flippers that rotate, a crowned forehead that looks similar to a dog's forehead, and ear flaps. They are air-breathing mammals, but they can hold their breath for up to ten minutes when they swim underwater. California sea lions eat squid, octopus, and fish. They live along the west coast of North America from Canada to Mexico, and also on the Galápagos Islands off South America.

Bighorn Sheep

Bighorn sheep (*Ovis canadensis*) usually give birth to their lambs in the spring. Within a few weeks the lambs form groups and only leave the groups to nurse from the mother ewes. Their name—bighorn sheep—comes from the adults' large horns. Both males and females grow horns, but males grow larger, distinctive curled horns. Bighorn sheep graze on the mountain vegetation of grasses; sedges, which are plants similar to grass; and forbs, which are broad-leafed flowering plants. They live in the mountain meadows, rocky mountain slopes and foothills of southwestern Canada, western United States, and northern Mexico.

Bactrian Camel *(back'-tree-an)*

Bactrian camel *(Camelus bactrianus)* calves are usually born in the spring. They are born with their eyes open. The three-foot-tall calves can stand within minutes of their birth and run within hours. Except for their two undeveloped humps, newborn calves look like miniatures of their parents. Their mothers care for them until they're four years old. Bactrian camels can go from a week to six months without drinking, but this has nothing to do with their humps. The two humps are composed of stored food energy—fat. The humps stand erect when the camels are well fed, but they flop over when the camels use the stored fat for nutrition. Bactrian camels are named after a part of Asia called Bactria, where they were likely tamed about three thousand years ago. Bactrian camels graze on grasses, but are known to eat a wide variety of food when they're hungry. These wild animals are an endangered species, and it's possible they could soon become extinct. Bactrian camels live on the plains, grasslands, and deserts of Mongolia and China.

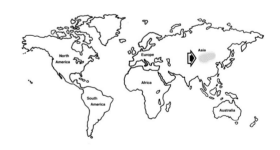

North American Beaver

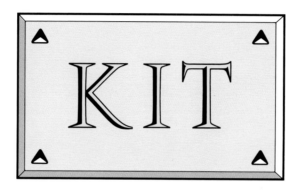

North American beaver *(Castor canadensis)* kits are born fully furred with their eyes open. They usually weigh from eight to twenty-two ounces. Beavers are nocturnal—active mostly at night—and are excellent swimmers. They have webbed hind feet, a paddle-like tail, and can stay underwater for up to five minutes. They are among the largest rodents and have chisel-like front teeth for gnawing on trees. They turn streams into ponds by using stones, mud, and logs that they cut to build dams. They also build lodges in the ponds, where they live and raise their kits. North American beavers eat the soft bark, leaves, and roots of trees such as willow, alder, birch, and aspen, as well as some aquatic plants like the young shoots of water lilies. They live in streams and ponds from northern Canada south to Mexico.

East Indian Red Jungle Fowl

East Indian red jungle fowl *(Gallus gallus murghi)* are the ancestors to the domestic fowl. They live in large flocks of up to fifty birds. When the chicks are only eight days old they can fly from branch to branch and at ten days old are able to fly a short distance with some degree of skill. East Indian red jungle fowl chicks primarily eat insects. As they grow into adults they also eat grains, fruits, and vegetables. They are native to the dry brush and tropical forests of East India.

New South Wales Wallaroo *(wall'-ah-roo)*

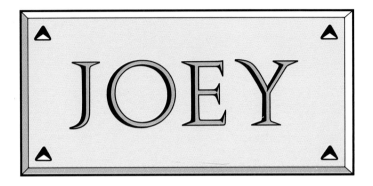

New South Wales wallaroos *(Macropus robustus robustus)* are medium-sized members of the kangaroo family. All kangaroos are marsupials—mammals with pouches. The joey lives in its mother's pouch. A New South Wales wallaroo joey holds onto its mother's nipple, which is located inside the pouch, and doesn't let go until it's a little over two months old. It peeks out from its mother's pouch when it's about five months old and first ventures out when it's a little more than six months old. But it doesn't leave its mother's pouch permanently until it's about eight months old. Wallaroos are nocturnal, feeding from dusk to dawn and resting during the day. New South Wales wallaroos can go without food or water for up to two or three months, longer than most other members of the kangaroo family. New South Wales wallaroos eat grasses, leaves, and herbs. They live on the mountains, on rough terrain, and in caves located in eastern Australia.

Yellow-backed Duiker *(die'-ker)*

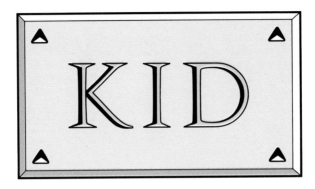

Yellow-backed duikers *(Cephalophus sylvicultor sylvicultor)* are called "bush goats" by the natives of Africa. Duikers are small-sized members of the antelope family, but the yellow-backed duiker is the largest of the duikers. Mothers give birth to a single kid, and the newborn stays hidden in vegetation for weeks. At about a month, kids develop a yellow patch of fur on their lower back, and by ten months the distinctive back of yellow fur is fully developed. The kids, both male and female, eventually grow a pair of short, single-spike horns, no longer than their ears. Adults are shy and only occasionally venture into clearings. When startled, they dive into dense vegetation. That's how they got their name—duiker means "diving buck." Yellow-backed duikers feed on grasses, leaves, fruit, and sometimes insects, and small animals such as birds. They live in the dense tropical forests of central and western Africa.

24

North Chinese Leopard

North Chinese leopard *(Panthera pardus japonensis)* cubs are born fully furred with their eyes closed. Newborns usually weigh between fifteen and twenty ounces. The cubs are kept hidden until they start to follow their mother when they're almost two months old. The mother cares for her cubs until they're about a year and a half old. North Chinese leopards are nocturnal and seldom seen by people. During the day they hide in lairs and during the night they roam up to thirty miles. These long-haired, cold-climate leopards are good climbers. They ambush their prey, or stalk it until the prey is close, then quickly rush it. North Chinese leopards eat small deer, wild goats, wild pigs, birds, and other small mammals. They are an endangered species, and it's possible they could soon become extinct. North Chinese leopards come from northern China where they live in forests, thickets, and alpine meadows.

Black-tailed Prairie Dog

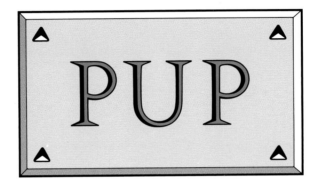

Black-tailed prairie dogs *(Cynomys ludovicianus)* are members of the squirrel family. They build extensive burrows with an elevated entrance to keep out water. Pups are born and raised in the burrows and don't appear aboveground until they're five or six weeks old. They stop nursing by the time they're seven weeks old. These highly social rodents live in groups called towns and form smaller groups within the towns, called wards. These wards have even smaller groups of about eight animals, called coteries. They kiss, nuzzle, groom, and play with each other. Adults defend their territory with a combined motion and call—a jump-yip. They then seek refuge in their burrows. Black-tailed prairie dogs maintain a rotating pasture and feed on herbs and grasses. They live on grassy prairies from south central Canada to north central Mexico.

Masai Giraffe *(mah-sigh')*

Masai giraffe *(Giraffa camelopardalis tippelskirchi)* calves fall five feet to the ground from their tall mother when they're born. The mother immediately licks her stunned newborn. It can weigh from one hundred to one hundred fifty pounds, and the six-foot-tall calf can first stand twenty minutes after being born. It stays with its mother for fifteen to eighteen months. A calf follows its mother everywhere, mimicking its mother's behavior. Giraffes have the same number of neck vertebrae—neck bones—as humans, but the vertebrae are elongated, which make giraffes the tallest terrestrial animal. Giraffes also have knobby horns that are like no other mammals'. Their name comes from the Arab word, *xirapha*, which means "the one that walks very fast." They can run thirty-five miles per hour. Masai giraffes eat leaves and buds from trees and bushes. They live on the tree-dotted African plains and open forests of southern Kenya and Tanzania.

European Mouflon *(moof'-lawn)*

European mouflon *(Ovis orientalis musimon)* lambs are born in the spring. Multiple births are common. As they mature, both males and females grow horns. Adult males weigh about seventy pounds and are larger than the females. European mouflon are the smallest of the wild sheep. They are the ancestors of our domestic sheep, which were domesticated in the eastern Mediterranean about ten thousand years ago. They have a woolly winter underfur that stays well-hidden by a coarse heavy coat. European mouflon eat grasses, herbs, and leaves. They live on the rocky mountains and grassy mountain meadows located on the Mediterranean islands of Sardinia, Corsica, and Cyprus.

Spider Monkey

Spider monkey *(Ateles geoffroyi geoffroyi)* mothers usually give birth to one baby then wait three years before giving birth to another. Babies spend much of their time playing, exploring, and wrestling with each other. Spider monkeys have strong arms, long legs, and long prehensile tails—tails that can grasp. They can hang by their hands, feet, or tails. They can even pick up things with their tails. Spider monkeys live in treetops, can easily swing through the forest, and are able to jump over thirty feet from tree to tree. They often groom each other. Spider monkeys mostly eat fruit, but they also eat nuts, seeds, buds, flowers, leaves, insects, and eggs. They live in the tops of trees located in tropical forests from Mexico south through Central America to Colombia.

What is a baby?

A baby is a very young animal. The term *baby* can refer to any young animal, but it expressly applies to primates. These are most of the specific English names for the young in the animal kingdom.

Young Name	Animal Species
Baby	Chimpanzee, baboon, gibbon, gorilla, human, and monkey. *Refers to any young animal, specifically to primates.*
Calf	Antelope *(also called kid)*, buffalo, camel, domestic cow, dolphin, elephant, elk, giraffe, hippopotamus, okapi, moose, rhinoceros, takin, walrus, whale, and yak.
Caterpillar	Butterfly and moth.
Cheeper	Grouse, partridge, and quail.
Chick	Domestic fowl. *Most birds.*
Colt	Young male horse *(also called a foal)*.
Cub	Brown, black, grizzly, panda, polar, spectacled, and sun bear; cheetah, cougar, jaguar, leopard, lion, panther, and tiger; fox *(also called kit or pup)*, and shark. *Larger members of the cat family are called cubs. Smaller members of the cat family are called kittens. (Koalas are marsupials, not bears, and are often mistakenly referred to as cubs. Young koalas are called joeys.)*
Cygnet	Swan.
Duckling	Duck.
Eaglet	Eagle.
Elver	Eel.
Eyas	Hawk.
Fawn	Deer and gazelle.
Filly	Young female horse *(also called a foal)*.
Fingerling	Fish *(also called fry)*.
Fledgling	*Chicks who are beginning to grow their flight feathers. See also nestling and other specific birds, such as duckling, eaglet, eyas, gosling, and pigeon.*
Foal	Ass, donkey, horse *(a young male horse is also called a colt and a young female horse is also called a filly)*, and zebra.
Fry	Fish *(also called fingerling)*.

Young Name	Animal Species
Gosling	Goose.
Hatchling	Turtle.
Joey	Kangaroo, koala, wallaby, and wallaroo. *A joey is a marsupial and also may be called a pouchling.*
Kid	Antelope *(also called a calf)*, domestic goat, ibex, and Rocky Mountain goat.
Kit	Beaver, fox *(also called a cub or pup)*, raccoon, skunk, and rabbit. *("Bunny" is an informal name for a rabbit, young or old.)*
Kitten	Domestic cat. fishing cat, lynx, ocelot, and serval *(also called a cub). Smaller members of the cat family are called kittens.*
Lamb	Domestic sheep and mouflon.
Larva	Insect.
Leveret	Hare.
Nestling	*A bird that has not grown enough to leave its nest. Compare to fledgling.*
Nymph	Dragonfly.
Piglet	Boar, domestic pig *(also called a shoat)*, and warthog.
Polliwog	Frog *(also called a tadpole)*.
Pouchling	Kangaroo, koala, wallaby, and wallaroo. *A pouchling, a young marsupial, is also called a joey.*
Poult	Turkey.
Pup	Coyote, dingo, domestic dog, fox *(also called a cub and a kit)*, jackal, otter, prairie dog, sea lion, seal, squirrel, and wolf. *Some pups are also called whelps.*
Shoat	Domestic pig *(also called a piglet)*.
Spiderling	Spider.
Squab	Pigeon.
Tadpole	Frog *(also called a polliwog)*.
Whelp	Dingo, domestic dog, jackal, and wolf. *A whelp is also called a pup.*

In this book, the name of the young that accompanies each photo is the preferred name for that species. For a name to be included in the list above, a minimum of three references was required. This list of names was compiled from many sources, including English dictionaries; English encyclopedias; *Walker's Mammals of the World*, 4th edition, by Ronald M. Nowak and John L. Paradiso, The Johns Hopkins University Press, 1983; *Biological Values for Selected Mammals* by Zwerling, et al., The San Francisco Zoological Society, January 1983; *The Encyclopedia of Mammals*, edited by David MacDonald, Facts on File, 1984; and from interviews with zookeepers and zoo officials at the Saint Louis Zoo, Saint Louis, Missouri; the San Diego Zoo, San Diego, California; and the Taronga Zoo, Sydney, Australia.

Many times there is more than one name for the young of an animal species. For example, the young of frogs are called tadpoles or polliwogs. Also, a name can apply to more than one animal species. For example, a pup could describe the young of a California sea lion; a black-tailed prairie dog, which is a member of the squirrel family; and also a domestic dog. Yet for many animal species there is no specific English word for the young.

Names for the young of various animal species reflect the culture where that language developed. For example, horses have been prevalent in English-speaking countries, so in the English language there is not only a name for a young horse—foal—but also a specific name for a young male horse—colt—and a young female horse—filly.

What is a zoo?

A zoo is a place where children and adults observe and learn about many animal species—from aracaris to matamatas to zebras. A well-designed zoo is a place for the recreation of the people who visit it, as well as for the wild animals who live there.

A zoo has an even more important function. It's also a modern-day ark—a place for conserving animal species in a race against extinction. Many species face extinction because of the loss of wildlife habitat and overhunting. A zoo provides a place where a species can live and reproduce. At the same time, it provides a place where the public can learn about the need to preserve wildlife habitats. If a species has become extinct in the wild, breeding programs at zoos enable the remaining members of that endangered species to reproduce and, hopefully, to be released back into the wild.

Mhorr gazelle fawn
(Gazella dama mhorr)
at the San Diego Zoo

For example, Mhorr gazelles used to live in the stony African deserts of Morocco and Senegal. This fawn at the San Diego Zoo is one of only about 125 Mhorr gazelles alive on our planet. Mhorr gazelles were hunted nearly to extinction. The few remaining animals were moved to Spain in the mid-1970s. This fawn is descended from that last remaining herd. The only population of Mhorr gazelles outside Europe is at the San Diego Zoo. The zoo started with four, and now there are twenty. For now, Mhorr gazelles can still be seen by the public, while they are managed in zoo breeding programs.

Cheetah cub
(Acinonyx jubatus)
at the Saint Louis Zoo

Not all zoo animals are on display. Despite the fact that cheetahs are difficult to breed in captivity, more than twenty-five cubs have been born at the Saint Louis Zoo's Cheetah Survival Center, and more than ninety at the San Diego Zoo. Most of this work and many of the cheetahs aren't seen by the public. Behind the scenes, each cheetah is logged onto a list kept by breeding zoos so that the zoos can track breeding and genetic lineage. This ensures a large gene pool and prevents species inbreeding. Programs like this are carried out for many species, with zoos exchanging animals for reproduction.

The goal of a zoo is to preserve wild animal species. To emphasize the wildlife aspect of animal species many zoos have recently stopped giving their animals pet names. According to the American Association of Zoological Parks and Aquariums, this is being done to promote the idea of the animal as a species and not as an individual—to remind the public that most zoo animals are wildlife creatures, not domestic pets. While a few people may have been bothered by this new zoo policy, it appears the animals haven't minded it a bit.

PAGE	SPECIES NAME	YOUNG	ADULT FEMALE	ADULT MALE	COLLECTIVE NOUN
1	Northern koala	joey			
4–5	Bawean deer *	fawn	doe	buck	herd
6–7	Grevy's zebra *	foal	mare	stallion	herd
8–9	Fishing cat	kitten			
10–11	Spectacled bear *	cub			
12–13	California sea lion	pup	cow	bull	herd
14–15	Bighorn sheep	lamb	dam or ewe	buck or ram	flock or herd
16–17	Bactrian camel *	calf	cow	bull	herd
18–19	North American beaver	kit			family

PAGE	SPECIES NAME	YOUNG	ADULT FEMALE	ADULT MALE	COLLECTIVE NOUN
20–21, 40	East Indian red jungle fowl	chick	hen	cock or rooster	flock
22–23	New South Wales wallaroo	joey	doe or flier	buck or boomer	herd or troop or mob
24–25	Yellow-backed duiker	kid			herd
26–27	North Chinese leopard *	cub			
28–29	Black-tailed prairie dog	pup			town or ward or coterie
30–31	Masai giraffe	calf	cow	bull	herd
32–33	European mouflon	lamb	dam or ewe	buck or ram	flock or herd
34–35	Spider monkey	baby	mother	father	band

*Vulnerable, threatened, or endangered species.

(These three categories of species are in order of least to most endangered for extinction.)

No enclosure needed for this zoo animal

East Indian red jungle fowl chicks *(Gallus gallus murghi)* roam freely about the San Diego Zoo with their parents and, by eating insects, the chicks help to control the insect population. Human children *(Homo sapiens)* also roam freely about the zoo with their parents, but they eat other foods.

Photo-illustrating *The Baby Zoo*

Patience was the major ingredient. For example, after waiting three days for the rain to clear, more than ten hours over a span of three additional days was spent observing and photographing the zebra foal. For the best photograph, most of the animals could only be photographed at a certain time of day, due to the location of their enclosures in relation to the sun.

The zookeepers were invaluable aides. They advised me as to when the animals were most active. Many times, for example, with the shy yellow-backed duiker kid and the Grevy's zebra foal, the keepers arranged feeding times so that I was able to photograph the animals when they came out to a scenic location in their enclosure.

My favorite time for photographing was at the end of the day, just after the zoo closed. The animals, curious and active in the quiet of dusk, were fascinating to watch. In the golden light of day's end, it was just me and the animals. After spending so much time simply observing, I felt a certain bond with them.

The Baby Zoo was photo-illustrated using a Nikon F4 camera with 24mm, 85mm, 180mm, 300mm, and 600mm Nikkor lenses. The film used was Kodachrome 64 processed by Kodalux.